Old COATBRIDGE

by
Oliver van Helden

A propaganda-laden tram photographed at the Coatbridge Depot in Main Street, encouraging men to enlist to fight in the First World War.

ISBN 1 84033 116 X

FURTHER READING

The books listed below were used by the author during his research. None of them are available from Stenlake Publishing. Those interested in finding out more are advised to contact their local bookshop or reference library.

Coatbridge – Three Centuries of Change, Peter Drummond and James Smith, Monklands Library Services, 1982.
The Monklands – An Illustrated Architectural Guide, Allan Peden, RIAS, 1992.
Ordnance Gazetteer of Scotland, ed. Francis H. Groome, Thomas C. Jack, 1885.
The Origins of the Scottish Railway System, 1722-1844, C. J. A. Robertson, John Donald, 1983.
The Rise and Progress of Coatbridge, Andrew Miller, 1864.
Slater's Directory of Scotland, 1910.
Statistical Account of Scotland, 1793.
New Statistical Account of Scotland, 1840.
Third Statistical Account of Scotland, 1951.
Tramways of the Monklands, Ian L. Cormack, The Scottish Tramway Museum Society.
Airdrie and Coatbridge Luminary.
Airdrie and Coatbridge Advertiser.

ACKNOWLEDGEMENTS

Thanks to Robert Grieves for providing the pictures on pages 40, 41 and the back cover. Special thanks to the Rev. Jim Allan, and to George and Sadie Allan, for sharing their memories of old Coatbridge with me and providing a lot of additional information.

Donaldson's shop is listed in *Slater's Directory of Scotland* for 1910, and stood at 5 Gartsherrie Road. The same premises are visible in the picture on page 36, where they can be located by the barber's pole in the terrace of shops on the right.

INTRODUCTION

Lying in the heart of a populous and manufacturing county, and on the great road betwixt the two chief cities of the kingdom, this parish furnishes ample room for statistical observations.

When the Rev. John Bower wrote these words about Old Monkland Parish in 1793, most of the people that he ministered to earned their living from agriculture or handloom weaving. But 23 years previously an Act of Parliament had been obtained for the cutting of the Monkland Canal, and when completed this new means of moving goods to and from Glasgow changed the landscape of the parish and the lives of its parishioners beyond recognition. It took some time for the influence of the canal to be felt, but by the beginning of the nineteenth century it was beginning to take effect.

There was nothing ambiguous about the canal's purpose, which was 'to open an easy communication with the interior parts of the country, and by reducing the price of coal, to be of advantage to the manufacturers of Glasgow'. The abundant coal reserves of Old Monkland Parish (and subsequently New Monkland) became gold mines for those that owned or leased the land below which they lay, because for the first time minerals could be transported to the rich city markets with ease.

Wherever possible, pits were sunk next to the canal so that coal could be transferred onto barges with the minimum of effort. In *The Rise and Progress of Coatbridge*, Andrew Miller described how: 'in 1793, four collieries were established along the banks of the canal. . . . In these four collieries upwards of 400 men were employed, who, by their labour, produced, at a rough estimate, upwards of 200,000 carts of coal annually, or about 130,000 tons.' When new workings were begun on the Drumpellier estate in 1826 'the pits were sunk close to the side of the water; the coal being emptied from the hutches as they came out of the pits down the screens into the boats, thus combining economy with despatch'. The new workings fuelled a rapid population growth, and the number of people living in Old Monkland increased from 1,813 in 1755 to 9,580 in 1831.

Two important factors led to the prodigious growth of iron-making in the Monkland parishes in the early nineteenth century. One of these was the discovery of a seam of ironstone that became known as blackband, described as containing 'so much coal as nearly to burn itself'. The other was J. B. Neilson's discovery that preheating air before passing it through blast furnaces dramatically increased the efficiency of the iron-smelting process. According to Miller: 'the fruits of this important discovery [the

hot blast] soon evinced themselves in the district, by the extension of the existing works at Calder and Gartsherrie, and in the erection of new works at Dundyvan, Calderbank, Summerlee, Carnbroe, and Langloan.' Coatbridge's iron era had arrived.

Following the success of the canal, railway lines were built to open up new mineral fields and cash in on the profitable monopoly that the canal was enjoying. The first such line was the Monkland and Kirkintilloch Railway (opened in 1826), which was later augmented by the Ballochney, and Wishaw and Coltness Railways. The upstart Garnkirk and Glasgow Railway opened in 1831 and ran parallel to the canal, competing with it directly. Such was the impact of these new railway routes that in February 1840 Rev. William Thomson wrote: 'The canal rates have been reduced since the introduction of railways nearly one-third, and yet the revenue is in a thriving condition'. A gazetteer of 1885 described Coatbridge as standing 'in the midst of a perfect network of railways'.

In the early 1830s the town of Coatbridge was formally established when the Baird family, owners of Gartsherrie Ironworks, laid out the principal streets, plus buildings including the Coatbridge Inn and Gartsherrie Church. Coatbridge became the focal point for a number of adjacent villages including Gartsherrie, Whifflet and Langloan. By the late nineteenth century the town was synonymous with heavy industry and pollution, as the *Ordnance Gazetteer of Scotland* of 1885 described: 'Fire, smoke, and soot, with the roar and rattle of machinery, are its leading characteristics; the flames of its furnaces cast on the midnight sky a glow as if of some vast conflagration'. It went on to say that: 'Everywhere are heard the brattling of machinery, the sonorous stroke of mighty hammers, and the hissing and clanking of the steam-engine'.

In 1840 William Thomson noted that: 'Out of the eighty-eight furnaces for the manufacture of iron, which at present exist in Scotland, sixty-five are in this parish, or in its immediate neighbourhood.' But the intensive concentration of iron-making in such a small area couldn't be sustained indefinitely, and 24 years later Andrew Miller described supplies of blackband ironstone as 'now nearly exhausted'. By the end of the First World War there were only five ironworks left, and many of these closed soon afterwards: Langloan in 1919; Calder and Carnbroe in 1921; and Summerlee in 1929. The last ironworks, Gartsherrie, lasted until 1967. Today the legacy of Coatbridge's industrial past is remembered at Summerlee Heritage Park, but the heavy industries have all but gone.

Coatbridge's largest ironworks were Summerlee and Gartsherrie, and this picture and the one opposite were probably taken at one of these works. The dome-topped vessels in this picture are hot blast stoves. J. B. Neilson's hot-blast process significantly increased the efficiency of iron smelting by directing a heated flow of air into the base of the furnaces. The airflow worked on the same principle as bellows, introducing greater quantities of oxygen into the furnace and encouraging the coking coal that was dropped in from the top (along with an approximately equal measure of crushed ironstone), to burn. The burning coke produced heat and carbon monoxide, which combined with the iron ore to produce molten iron and carbon dioxide. Hot blast stoves contained a latticework of bricks and a furnace which heated them to a very high temperature. Once this had been reached, air was pumped through the stoves, where it was heated by the bricks before being piped into a blast furnace. In 1895 Summerlee had seven blast furnaces, four of which were 72 feet high and three of which measured 57 feet.

The ramp in this picture was used to hoist coke and ironstone to the top of the blast furnace behind it (an identical ramp, possibly the same one, is visible towards the left of the picture opposite). Working in close proximity to a furnace was understandably uncomfortable, and Andrew Miller described the characteristics of the men who did this job: 'Blast furnacemen have always been easily distinguished from the rest of the community, by the peculiar red and scorched appearance of their faces, caused by the intense heat to which they are exposed, a heat which creates in them a great thirst, and often a desire to quench it in something stronger than water.' Iron produced in the furnace collected in molten form and was regularly run off into moulds, where it solidified. This cast or 'pig' iron was brittle, and whilst suitable for some purposes, such as making household ranges, generally underwent further melting and working to produce more useful malleable iron.

The Baird family, who founded Gartsherrie Ironworks (above), were farmers whose industrial careers began when they leased a coalfield at Rochsolloch, where coal was reached from 'a day level [drift mine] and a gin pit'. They moved from coal-mining to iron-making in the late 1820s, audaciously flouting Neilson's patent rights to the hot blast, for which they were subsequently forced to pay substantial damages. By that time, however, they had become so well-established that the compensation sought was essentially trifling, and their Gartsherrie works continued operating for another 150 years (until 1967). Unlike the ramp mechanism used to raise coke and ironstone to the furnace-tops in the previous picture, a more modern winding gear is in place here. The wheels of at least one winding engine can be seen protruding from the top of the rectangular brick tower to the centre-left. A similar arrangement was used at the Summerlee works in 1895 when an observer noted that: 'two cages are provided in square brick towers for raising the material'.

Small locomotives, known as pug engines, were the workhorses of Coatbridge's heavy industries, and the major works had networks of tracks used by these locomotives to fetch and carry raw materials and finished products. This one, which belonged to William Baird & Co., was photographed at Gartsherrie in 1929. As early as 1793, the author of the *Statistical Account* for Old Monkland Parish noticed the benefits that steam power was bringing to the district, when he wrote of the Fullarton coal workings that: 'A large steam engine drains a field of 800 acres. The coals are carried out of the pit by a machine, in place of a horse-gin.' Whilst having great benefits, steam power was also dangerous, as Andrew Miller described in *Rise and Progress*: 'From the immense steam power required for machinery in the manufacture of malleable iron, boiler explosions of a very serious and destructive character have occurred, by which many lives have been sacrificed.'

The Gartsherrie Institute was built by the Bairds and included swimming baths, plus a hall where dances and other social events took place. The different areas of Coatbridge maintained distinct identities, and the community at Gartsherrie was very close-knit. Following its demolition, houses were built on the site of the institute around the time of the Second World War. Well into the twentieth century, many houses in Coatbridge still had very basic sanitary arrangements, and new public baths opened in Main Street in 1938. As well as washing facilities, these provided 'swimming, Turkish and Russian baths'. Much of the housing in Coatbridge was provided by the various works for their employees, and was of very poor quality. Company houses tended to be built near the works they belonged to, which meant that as well as being cramped they were often situated near belching chimneys.

A pug belonging to Calder Ironworks, one of the first ironworks to be established in Coatbridge. Immigration went hand-in-hand with the area's rapid industrialisation, and as iron-making had begun at other locations in Scotland prior to its reaching Coatbridge, skilled workers from sites such as Carron, Omoa and Muirkirk were brought in to man William Dixon's Calder works when they became operational in the early 1800s. When malleable iron began to be made at Dundyvan and Calderbank ironworks, Andrew Miller wrote that: 'the skilled workmen required were brought chiefly from the iron manufacturing districts of England and Wales, the greatest numbers being from Staffordshire'. An incoming workforce was necessary to man the new labour-hungry industries, and as early as 1840 Rev. William Thomson observed of his parish that: 'A great many Irish are everywhere to be found.'

An unidentified picture of one of Coatbridge's many ironworks, situated on the banks of the Monkland Canal with several barges visible in the foreground. One of the first factories to be established on the canal bank was 'a large brick and tyle work, where are manufactured blue, pan, and slate tyles', which dated from 1785. This extract from the *Airdrie and Coatbridge Advertiser* of 2 April 1859 illustrates how dangerous the new industrial workplaces could be: 'SERIOUS ACCIDENT. On Saturday, a young woman of the name of Agnes M'Ginnis, while employed making tiles at Coats' brickwork, got her hand cut off. She had been working at a machine for making tiles, and unconsciously allowed her hand to come in contact with the machine. It was drawn in and horribly mutilated, so much so that amputation above the wrist was considered necessary.'

In 1793, the Rev. John Bower boasted of 'the vast number of gentlemen's houses with which the parish is adorned, many of them finished in the greatest taste'. Drumpellier belonged to the Glasgow tobacco baron Andrew Buchanan, who bought the estate in 1735 and began work on the house in 1741. Minerals were worked on the estate, and there was an underground fire at Drumpellier No. 9 pit in 1851, which started in the flues of a furnace being used to fire a steam engine at the bottom of the shaft. Drumpellier Cricket Club was established in 1850, and the club – along with Drumpellier Golf Club – continues to thrive. During the First World War the house served as an auxiliary hospital, and in 1951, when the *Third Statistical Account* was written, it was being used as the golf club house. It has since been demolished.

Langloan terminus, with the junction of Woodside Street to the right. The two-storey house on the left was formerly the home of Dr James Sweeney, a local GP. He drove a Daimler, which apart from being a curiosity in its own right had the added fascination of a sign in the back window that could be illuminated to read 'THANK YOU', and was lit up for courteous drivers. On 28 December 1923 Airdrie and Coatbridge's trams were linked with Glasgow's when the first car ran from the city to Langloan terminus along the newly built track from Baillieston.

The buildings in the background on the left of this picture stood in Bank Street, and included McIver's cabinet maker's shop and a doctor's surgery. Cullen Street branched off Bank Street at the same point, and the stables for Rankin's dairy were located there. When English ironworkers were brought to the district in the 1830s, their new employers built houses for them in the style that they had been used to in England. These were described as consisting of 'long ranges of two storied tenements, each family having four apartments'. The new skilled workers were in demand, and earned good wages, although Andrew Miller said of them that: 'the majority were very illiterate, purse proud, and arrogant, quarrelsome and over-bearing towards the other working classes, which led to frequent brawls and fighting'.

This picture shows the house of Coatbridge's erstwhile poet, Janet Hamilton, who lived at Langloan and died on 30 Octobér 1873. Described as 'a poor shoemakers wife', she was the mother of a large family and had married at 13. She didn't begin to compose poetry until at least the age of 50, and as she couldn't write had to compose in her head and remember her verses until her husband or son was able to write them down for her. This ultimately led her to devise her own method of writing, unintelligible to others but sufficient to relieve the strain on her memory until someone could transcribe the verses for her. The house was demolished many years ago.

Janet Hamilton's funeral service was conducted in the Free Church, and she was buried in Old Monkland churchyard. Reporting on the funeral, the *Advertiser* described her as 'certainly one of the most remarkable Scotch women of the present century'; her popularity was reflected by the cortege of over 400 people that turned out for the event, and the building of this memorial, erected in 1880. The newspaper also paid tribute to 'the noble services rendered by the poetess to the cause of temperance by her vehement denunciation of "the curse of Scotland" '.

Reverend Bower considered the land in Old Monkland Parish to be of superior agricultural quality to that of neighbouring New Monkland, although he did admit that the mineral fields below the surface were more extensive in the other parish. By the middle of the nineteenth century, Coatbridge's rural population had become a minority, as Rev. Thomson noted in 1840: 'Nearly the whole population, with the exception of those connected with rural operations, and a few weavers and other necessary tradesmen, are absorbed in the coal and iron trade'. Nonetheless, the farms that surrounded the town remained vital for supplying foodstuffs to its inhabitants. While horses remained important in agriculture and general transport well into the twentieth century, Andrew Miller wrote that: 'At every work, or even colliery, railway locomotives are doing duty in working the traffic at which horses were previously employed.' James Thomson of 30 Crichton Street is listed under 'Dairymen and Cow Keepers' in a 1910 trade directory, and this cart may have belonged to the same firm at an earlier date.

Bank Street, with the junction of Hutton Street to the right. A. B. Brown's tearoom is just out of shot to the left. The west end of Coatbridge was the original centre of the village, probably because of its proximity to Old Monkland Parish Church, 'a large and commodious house' which was rebuilt in 1790. According to Andrew Miller, a postmaster called Alexander Morrison was appointed in Langloan in 1833 (prior to that the nearest post town had been Airdrie). However, at about the same time the Baird family were engaged in laying out Coatbridge's principal streets with landmarks such as Gartsherrie Church and the Coatbridge Inn. In 1836, in response to a petition 'signed by a number of influential gentlemen', the post office was moved to Coatbridge proper.

The two-storey building on the left of this picture of Bank Street stood at number 18 and was built of red brick. It initially housed the Poor Law offices, which later became Welfare Services and subsequently the Social Work Department. Asides from a variety of pubs, one of the more notable shops in the terrace on the right was Mills & Co. which sold sheet music and 78s and was the only music shop in town.

COATBRIDGE, BANK STREET, LOOKING WEST.

The Coatbridge Cinema opened in 1913 and was the town's first purpose-built cinema. It had very long rows, and the view of the screen from the end of these wasn't very good. The single-storey shop to the left of the cinema was Brownlie's grain store and grocers. Agnew and Harrow's garage at 28 Bank Street was agents for Ford, and also Angus-Sanderson cars, which were made in Newcastle.

The shop under the bridge next to Eadie's was a sweet shop, and the single-storey building beyond it was used as a store by Kirk's plumbers. Gibson's ironmongers adjoined this, and between them, obscured by the tram, was the shop where George Allan had his shoemaking business. The bus on the right is turning into Ross Street.

By the late 1920s, Alexander Lees had already built up a substantial business in Coatbridge, with grocery shops at four locations in the town (Bank Street, Main Street, Buchanan Street and Dundyvan Road), as well as a confectioners at a different address in Bank Street (number 137). Lees became world-famous for their macaroon bars and snowballs, which are now exported all over the globe. A jingle for an old TV ad went 'Lees, Lees, if you please, ask for Lees on bended knees'. The company continues to flourish and has a new factory in Calder Street.

The Caledonian railway station, known as the 'Caley', was entered through the grand building on the left with the canopy (now Pullman's bar and restaurant). Its near neighbour, operated by the North British Railway, was named Coatbridge Central and closed to passenger traffic on 10 September 1951. The town's rapid growth during the nineteenth century led to an enormous strain on its resources, and Andrew Miller wrote that a water supply initially depended on: 'the precarious supplies from a few wells in the neighbourhood, several of which during the drought of summer [regularly] failed'. Worse still, canal water was used for human consumption, and Miller describes how there was often a water shortage when the canal was drained for repair work during the summer, with the public resorting to collecting the muddy dregs from the bottom.

The Bairds built the Coatbridge Inn (shown here as the Royal Hotel) and an adjoining row of shops in 1835. Coatbridge experienced cholera outbreaks in 1832 and 1848, and during the latter epidemic daily meetings were held at the inn so that doctors could assess the progress of the disease and what should be done about it. A special hospital was set up on the south side of the canal by the brick and tile works, whilst other measures were taken to try and stem the spread of the disease: 'Houses were fumigated, and white-washed; quantities of tar were poured out upon the streets, and set fire to, and all measures adopted, that human skill could suggest, to purify the tainted atmosphere'. Poor quality housing probably contributed to poor health in the district, as this 1864 description suggests: 'often large families are huddled together into one small apartment; of all ages and sex, in sickness or in disease, the whole family are accommodated under the same roof, breathing the close, sickening, and, it may be, tainted atmosphere.'

The building that adjoined the Coatbridge Inn, with the turret on its roof, became a pub called Wheeltappers and Shunters, which is still in business today (it was previously the Tower Bar). Wheeltappers checked the wheels of trains when they were at stations; the noise a wheel made when it was tapped with a metal bar changed if it was cracked, and having been identified a faulty and potentially dangerous wheel could be replaced. In 1920 the three-storey Airdrie Savings Bank was built on the site of the Coatbridge Inn. The original location (above) of the Whitelaw Fountain marked the spot where a level crossing connecting Gartsherrie Ironworks with the malleable ironworks on the canal bank crossed Main Street. The fountain was inaugurated on 10 August 1875, and on the previous Saturday the *Advertiser* reported that: 'the merchants of the town and most of the public works in the locality have agreed to have a half-day holiday on the occasion'. The ceremony was scheduled for 3 p.m., with music provided by the band of the 18th Light Infantry from Glasgow, and was to be followed by a banquet in the Theatre Royal at five o'clock.

The branch of the canal in the foreground of this picture led to Gartsherrie Ironworks. There was a basin at this point, below the station, where coal was transported from barges to railway waggons for transport onwards. The former North British Railway line can be made out running parallel to Sunnyside Road, and the long single-storey building to the right is the station building of Coatbridge Central.

Sunnyside Road, Coatbridge.

The Sunnyside Bar stood at the corner of Baird Street on Sunnyside Road, opposite the railway line. When he wrote the *Statistical Account* for Old Monkland Parish in 1793, Rev. John Bower expressed opinions on the evils of drink that were common amongst his peers in other parishes. He observed that: 'There are no less than 30 inns or public-houses in the parish. These, it must be confessed, are attended with the most pernicious effects to the health and morals of the people.'

Coatbridge's Temperance Halls were situated at 27 and 28 Sunnyside Road and are marked on the 1860 Ordnance Survey map next to a building called the Star Hotel. In *Rise and Progress*, published in 1864, Andrew Miller notes that the town's Total Abstinence Society had been formed 26 years previously, which would date its establishment to 1832. He goes on to say that: 'In 1847 the members built a large and commodious hall, which cost upwards of £500, and which holds about 500 people. It is fitted up with a platform and two rooms leading off from it'. In 1847 the *Advertiser* reported on a talk that was given at the temperance halls, at the end of which fourteen people, described as 'moderate drinkers', came forward and took the pledge. The former halls are visible in the picture on page 25, where they have 'COATBRIDGE (CENTRAL)' painted across them.

Most of the buildings on the right-hand side of Main Street have been flattened. The Circle Bar got its name because of its location on the gushet site at the end of Main Street and East Canal Street (which leads off to the right). The Whitelaw Fountain has been moved three times since its inauguration in August 1875, and a bleak roundabout with a security camera on it now stands in its place at this busy junction. There used to be a metal cup on a chain at each of the four basins round the fountain, where passers-by could help themselves to a drink from the continuously-flowing water supply. The tower to the right belonged to the old fire station.

This aerial picture, taken in 1929, shows Coatbridge's excellent transport infrastructure, which by this time centred around the railways and roads, rather than the canal. The Monkland and Kirkintilloch Railway opened in October 1826 and adjoining lines were quickly built to provide access to other mineral fields; the Ballochney Railway branched off the Monkland and Kirkintilloch in an easterly direction from Coatbridge, and the Wishaw and Coltness line extended south-east away from the town. These new lines meant that coal could be transported to Glasgow without using the Monkland Canal, but didn't compete directly with the canal as they used an indirect and hence longer route (the speed of rail transport compared to barge traffic compensated for the longer journey). When the Garnkirk and Glasgow Railway opened in 1831 the new line ran virtually parallel to the canal, offering a fast and cheap alternative means of getting coal to Glasgow, and severely damaging the canal's competitiveness. The railway caused an even greater upset by allowing traffic using the Wishaw and Coltness line to almost completely avoid the Monkland and Kirkintilloch Railway, costing the latter a lot of revenue.

Before Old Monkland became famous for iron-making, handloom weaving and agriculture were the principal sources of employment. In 1793 Rev. Bower wrote of the weavers that: 'there are no less than 400 in the parish, who all work to the manufacturers of Glasgow. They generally marry young, to which their high wages are an inducement.' The settlement that eventually grew to become Coatbridge was formed by the amalgamation of several adjacent villages, and hence the town grew up piecemeal. It was this that prompted the author of a gazetteer published in 1885 to remark that: 'the appearance of the whole, redeemed though it is by some good architectural features, is far more curious than pleasing.' Further along Main Street, shops, pubs and the Theatre Royal enjoyed views of ironworks ranged along the canal banks on the other side of the street.

MAIN STREET TO CROSS, COATBRIDGE

D 2800

The elegant four-storey building (centre) that was formerly Coia's Cafe currently lies empty. There was once a billiard hall in the basement, and the Coia family lived in the upper stories of the building.

MAIN STREET LOOKING TO CROSS, COATBRIDGE.   214571.

During the Second World War, Coatbridge's British Restaurant was situated in the terrace on the left. These government restaurants were set up to provide hearty meals at reasonable prices, and having chosen what you wanted and paid the cashier, you were given tokens to exchange for what you had ordered. Bobby Robertson's chemists was also in the row of shops on the left, and the Robertson family still have a pharmacy in Main Street. Water Street branched off Main Street at the near left, and led to the well-known BBs cinema. This was the cheapest picture house in town, something that was reflected in the standards of comfort inside!

Gartsherrie Academy was built by the Bairds in 1845 to educate the children of their workers, and cost £2,500. This picture shows it before additional classrooms were added to form a second floor over the flanking single-storey wings. After this extension there was a total of fifteen classrooms, which were arranged around a central hall. The windows overlooking the entrance were those of the headmaster's office, and in the days before co-education became the norm, boys used this entrance and girls used the one at the opposite end of the building. Having been boarded up for some time, the dilapidated academy building is now being redeveloped as luxury flats.

An early picture of Church Street taken before the post office was built at the bottom left-hand corner and the three-storey red sandstone Clydesdale bank appeared a few doors up on the right (according to Andrew Miller the Clydesdale opened a branch in the street in 1864). There was a pawnbrokers on the first floor of the building on the right-hand corner, and the traditional sign of three balls can be made out facing onto Main Street. The shop originally belonged to a Mr Waddell, and was taken over by his son-in-law Hugh Ross at the end of the nineteenth century.

The substantial building in the foreground on the left was formerly Coatbridge's post office. When the Middle Church, beyond it, burned down, its congregation moved to Drumpellier Church (now called the Middle Church). The former Gartsherrie Church (built by the Bairds), at the top of the street, is known locally as Mount Zion. According to the authors of *Coatbridge – Three Centuries of Change*, the Bairds were happy to provide land for Catholic and Episcopalian churches to be built in the town because they 'recognised the value of organised religion in keeping a certain social discipline among the work force'.

COATBRIDGE, CHURCH STREET FROM SUNNYSIDE STATION.

The stretch of road in the foreground of this picture is Gartsherrie Road, with Sunnyside Road crossing it where the car stands and Church Street continuing up the hill. The crossroads was called Sunnyside Cross, and the building on the near left corner was Chapman's pub. Dr Cordiner (senior) lived in one of the big villas near the top of Church Street on the right, and in later years his son Lindsay, a dentist, stayed across the road. In *The Monklands – An Illustrated Architectural Guide*, the two halves of Church Street are described as being 'lined with well-mannered bijou stone cottages and villas for the petit bourgeoisie'!

The central branch of Coatbridge Co-op was located in Muiryhall Street. With offices on the first floor, and a china shop, butchers and tobacconists downstairs, it typified the comprehensive range of services that local cooperative societies provided their members with.

The co-op's elegant drapery department stood at the corner of Muiryhall Street (right) and Dunbeth Road (left).

The Baxter's bus stands outside O'Donnel's pub on Main Street. Clifton Lane led between the pub and the barber's shop across from its doorway (the stripy pole can be made out on the right). This was where Matt Ballantyne carried on his trade, although because of his poor eyesight he was nicknamed 'the blin' barber'. The two-storey building in the background on the left was the Labour Exchange. Both the bikes have a white stripe painted on their rear mudguards, a measure that was introduced during the war to make cycling at night during blackouts slightly less dangerous.

Theatre Royal, Main Street, Coatbridge

Matt Ballantyne occupied the ground floor premises at the near corner of Coatbridge's grandiose Theatre Royal. This opened in 1875 as a theatre and opera house, but later staged variety shows and then became a cinema. It finally closed in August 1958, lying derelict for eight years before being demolished for road widening. An earlier theatre called the Adelphi opened in Coatbridge in 1863. The *Advertiser* of 26 September 1863 described it as 'a very substantial erection', adding that 'Lighted up brilliantly by gas, the house, looked at from the boxes, has really a surprisingly fine effect'. The theatre had opened on the previous Saturday to a full house, and the local paper said of its owners that: 'If they succeed in emptying the public houses several nights a week, they will effect an amount of good undreamt of in the philosophy of those who utterly condemn the stage.'

This bus belonged to John Carmichael's 'Highland' fleet, based at Greenfoot. John Carmichael was awarded the VC during the First World War after a grenade landed near him in the trench where he was stationed. On seeing it he took off his tin helmet, placed it over the grenade and stood on it. When the missile exploded he was wounded, but his bravery saved the lives of many of his fellow soldiers. A portion at the left-hand end of the Albion Rovers stand burned down in the 1940s or fifties and was never rebuilt.

Steele's pub is on the left of this picture, at the corner of Jackson Street. Granny Reid's small shop, housed in a shed, can be made out just beyond the billboard, with the pitched roof of the tram depot above and slightly to the right of it. Female tram conductors had a reputation for their no-nonsense manner when dealing with customers. On being asked politely whether there were any seats available on the upper deck, one of them replied with typical bluntness: 'Aye 34, and there's an arse on every one!'

Proposals for tram a service connecting Airdrie and Coatbridge were put forward as early as 1872, but it wasn't until February 1903 that work on a tramway was finally begun. The first car ran on 19 January 1904, and members of the two town councils and selected guests got the chance to ride on a tram for the first time on 5 February, when this picture was taken at Coatbridge Depot. Following speeches and refreshments, the guests travelled by tram to the Airdrie terminus at Motherwell Street. Reporting on matters the following day, the *Advertiser* applauded the new trams, observing that 'In these go-ahead days, people prefer riding in a car to walking'.

The village of Rosehall, which stood at the southern end of Whifflet Street, is now only remembered in the name Rosehall Avenue. This picture looks towards Whifflet and Coatbridge. On 18 February 1859 there was a fire at No. 5 pit, Rosehall Colliery. The *Advertiser* reported that it '[appeared to have] originated from an iron funnel, 40 fathoms long, which conveys the smoke up the pit from an engine at the bottom'. Two men volunteered to ascend the shaft to raise the alarm, following which pumps at the pit-head were used to direct water down it. The fire was put out and the men who were still at the pit bottom escaped without injury.

SHAWHEAD PITS Nº 3&4, WHIFFLET COATBRIDGE.

Coal waggons such as those in the right foreground held 10 to 15 tons, and a well-known expression went: 'Motherwell for coal and steel, Coatbridge for stealing coal.' Many people's houses backed on to railway lines, and drivers of goods trains regularly slowed down so that the guardsman could heave a raker of coal into his or a friend's back yard. (A raker was a large chunk of coal that hadn't been broken up into fire-sized pieces.)

An early view of The Whifflet, as people from this part of town always called it. The Big Tree pub, on the left corner, still serves as a landmark on Whifflet Street. Everything on the right has been demolished and the high-rise blocks of Whifflet Court and Calder Court stand on the site. Coatbridge became legendary for pollution at its industrial height, and it is said that you couldn't walk down the street in a white shirt without it quickly getting covered in soot from the local works.

Whifflet Street again, this time at the railway bridge on the approach to Coatbridge. Easton Place, a square of about 20 houses, stood below and to the right of the bridge. In the *New Statistical Account* for Old Monkland, Whifflet is listed as having 'three ironstone pits, and two coal-pits, containing the splint and black-band.' The author described splint coal as being 'of very superior quality', and went on to say that: 'This seam, when of any considerable thickness, is justly esteemed when got by the proprietors here a great prize.'

THE PUBLIC PARK, WHIFFLET.

John Bower wrote of his parish that: 'Contrary to what one would imagine, the people are healthy, and live long'. This seems surprising considering the severe pollution that the people of Coatbridge endured, and in the densely populated town small parks such as the one in Whifflet were amongst the only open spaces. The park is much the same today, although the bowling pavilion has been replaced by a new building and the swings to its left have gone. The drinking fountain that was erected at Coatdyke in 1886 to celebrate Coatbridge having become a burgh the previous year has now found its way into the park, probably because it had become a hindrance to traffic at its former location.

Coatdyke Main Street. In *Rise and Progress*, published in 1864, Andrew Miller observed that: 'Coatbridge, although entitled from its population and position to rank as a burgh . . . is still, from want of spirit or something else . . . neither a burgh on the roll Parliamentary nor Royal.' In fact, local industrialists discouraged the town from becoming a burgh because this would have required the introduction of pollution controls that were detrimental to profit. It has been said that one of their tactics was to try and keep Coatbridge as a collection of villages, although in 1885 they lost their struggle. When the area was ravaged by cholera in March 1832, Coatdyke was listed as one of the places that was worst affected.